THE ST. FRANCIS HOLY FOOL
PRAYER BOOK

THE
St.Francis
HOLY FOOL

Prayer Book

BY
JON M. SWEENEY

PARACLETE PRESS
BREWSTER, MASSACHUSETTS

2017 First Printing

The St. Francis Holy Fool Prayer Book

Copyright © 2017 by Jon M. Sweeney

ISBN 978-1-61261-830-2

All quotations from the Gospels and other parts of the New Testament are taken from *The New Jerusalem Bible*, published and copyright 1985 by Darton, Longman & Todd, Ltd. and Doubleday, a division of Random House, Inc., and used by permission of the publisher.

Scripture quotations from the Psalms are taken from the Book of Common Prayer and Administration of the Sacraments and Other Rites and Ceremonies of the Church according to the use of the Episcopal Church, copyright 1979 The Church Hymnal Corp., NY.

Scripture quotations from the songs and canticles and prophets of the Hebrew Scriptures are taken from the *New Revised Standard Version of the Bible*, copyright © 1993 and 1989 by the Division of Christian Education of the National Council of Churches of Christ in the USA. Used by permission. All rights reserved.

The Paraclete Press name and logo (dove on cross) are trademarks of Paraclete Press, Inc.

Library of Congress Cataloging-in-Publication Data
Names: Sweeney, Jon M., 1967- author.
Title: The St. Francis holy fool prayer book / Jon M. Sweeney.
Description: Brewster, Massachusetts : Paraclete Press, 2017. | Includes
  bibliographical references and index.
Identifiers: LCCN 2017017873 | ISBN 9781612618302 (pbk.)
Subjects: LCSH: Christian life—Catholic authors. | Catholic Church—
Prayers
  and devotions. | Francis, of Assisi, Saint, 1182-1226.
Classification: LCC BX2350.3 .S94 2017 | DDC 242/.802—dc23
LC record available at https://lccn.loc.gov/2017017873

10 9 8 7 6 5 4 3 2 1

Published by Paraclete Press
Brewster, Massachusetts
www.paracletepress.com

Printed in the United States of America

FOR THOSE WHO TRY TO LIVE THE GOSPEL,

AND BY SO DOING, FEEL LIKE FOOLS

CONTENTS

III
DAILY OFFICE
for HOLY FOOLS

IV

OCCASIONAL PRAYERS
FOR FOOLS

V
FOUR STORIES
of BROTHER JUNIPER
from *The Little Flowers*

HOW IT IS GOOD TO BE A FOOL

T will always remember the day I decided to introduce my preschool-age daughter to one of my favorite movies, *Singing in the Rain*, starring Gene Kelly, Donald O'Connor, and Debbie Reynolds. We sat and watched it together on the couch. She didn't wiggle much and laughed at the right places. I knew she was enjoying it.

But then we got to the title song and dance number. There was Gene Kelly, blissfully enjoying a rainstorm. You probably remember how he runs back and forth across a city street at nighttime in the pouring rain, singing at the top of his lungs, tap-dancing by stomping in puddles, grinning at a cop on patrol, becoming completely drenched in his business clothes. He is wearing a suit—and even gives away his umbrella!

As my daughter and I watched, I laughed out loud and was grinning ear to ear. That's what I always do when I watch that scene. She watched carefully, and was smiling, but to my surprise, she then turned to me in the middle of the scene and said, "That's kind of stupid, Dad."

She was only four at the time, but I was sort of offended. I don't know for certain why. Forget that she said the word "stupid" for a moment; we'll deal with that another day. Why was I bothered by her reaction? It isn't as if the movie has anything intimately or immediately to do with *me*, but I wanted her to like it as I did. "Why?" I implored. Then I suddenly realized that I probably knew what she meant by what she said. So I revised. "Do you mean . . . because he's getting all wet?"

"Yeah," she replied, still smiling, looking at the screen. The puddle-stomping continued even as we talked, and she was still trying to figure out the meaning of the scene. "But he's being kind of stupid," she added, yet again.

How do I answer this? I thought. *How do I get her to understand what this means?*

Adults easily understand that what Gene Kelly is doing is anything but stupid. But can his spirit be communicated in words? I at least gave it another try. "Not *stupid*, honey," I said. "Maybe he's just being . . . *foolish*."

Maybe.

A child can't really appreciate what "foolish" means, nor how being a fool can be a virtue, a really good thing. Nor can she appreciate how foolishness might be a healthy sign that something good is happening, or able to happen, in your life. After all, how could someone who is still innocently carefree most of the time—without real responsibilities or stress—understand the absolute delight that can come when we allow ourselves to "let loose" others' expectations? That's what Gene Kelly is doing by singing and dancing in the rain: allowing his joy to overcome his decorum. We adults know this, and that's why we love watching him do it. Probably, we are wishing, deep down, that we could do that too.

G. K. Chesterton wrote in *Orthodoxy*, "Angels can fly because they can take themselves lightly." We'd all like to fly like angels—or at least like Gene Kelly.

I might have communicated better with my daughter that day as we watched the movie together if I'd said that Gene Kelly was being "crazy." She sometimes likes to be "crazy" with her friends. They seem to know and appreciate that word for its sense of nonconformity and playfulness. But as an adult, "crazy" is a word that doesn't seem appropriate. I know how it means a lot of things, some clinical, and how sometimes it might be perceived as an insult, or at least out of place. That's why I quickly decided it wasn't the way to go when I was trying to explain why singing in the rain isn't necessarily "dumb."

I used the word "fool" instead, but then again, "fool" is also an insult to many. The word was even used that way—as a kind of insult—in the Hebrew Scriptures, as we will see in a second. But to many Christians throughout history, foolishness has been a goal, a spiritual occupation, even a badge of honor. They have gone out of their way to earn the name *fool*, even when they knew that those who were saying it never intended it as a compliment. They have been "fools for Christ's sake," to quote St. Paul, who says it like this:

Here we are, fools for Christ's sake, while you are the clever ones in Christ; we are weak, while you are strong; you are honored, while we are disgraced. To this day, we go short of food and drink and clothes, we are beaten up and we have no homes; we earn our living by laboring with our own hands; when we are cursed, we answer with a blessing; when we are hounded, we endure it passively; when we are insulted, we give a courteous answer (1 Cor. 4:10–13).

Otherwise known as *holy fools*.

This can be confusing and for good reasons. Even the Bible seems to contradict itself about fools. A fool for Christ's sake is altogether different from the kind of person the psalmist describes when he or she begins, "The fool says in his heart, 'There is no God.' They are corrupt, their deeds are vile; there is no one who does good. The Lord looks down from heaven on all mankind to see if there are any who understand, any who seek God. All have turned away, all have become corrupt; there is no one who does good, not even one" (Ps. 14:1–3). That's not a foolishness to emulate! Nevertheless, St. Paul's foolishness is. The Bible speaks about both kinds of fools—good and bad—but for the most part, the good sort has been lost.

THE GOOD FOOL

The foolishness praised by St. Paul is a way of living out Jesus's teachings in the Beatitudes. "Beatitude" comes from a Latin word that means *happiness*. These are ways to true happiness, and of course they aren't what you might expect. Who is blessed? The poor in spirit, the meek, the hungry and thirsty, people who are peacemakers—not the powerful. Even the "pure of heart"—and the phrase means pretty much what it implies, and that is, those who are simple or willingly naive—are singled out as blessed. Do you want to sign up for this sort of blessedness, happiness? Not many do. That's why we call them fools. *Holy* fools.

A Christian can point to Jesus's foolishness as the exemplar, just as Jesus sometimes pointed to the Hebrew prophets as his inspiration for defying others' expectations. Like Jeremiah, Jesus dressed simply. Like Isaiah, Jesus often walked around barefoot, and he didn't know where he was going to sleep at night. Contrary to what religious leaders thought appropriate, Jesus chose a strange mix of people as his followers and friends (women, the poor, despised tax collectors, the untouchable sick). Occasionally, he went against societal norms and theological expectations with an attitude of naiveté. No matter if someone thought he was "dumb."

Even Jesus's own family thought he was a fool at times—and not the good kind. Just after he appointed his twelve disciples, the Gospel of

Mark says: "He went home again, and once more such a crowd collected that they could not even have a meal. When his relations heard of this, they set out to take charge of him; they said, 'He is out of his mind'" (Mk. 3:21). In twenty-first-century language, that sounds like they staged an intervention! They wanted to set him straight. Perhaps he was embarrassing the family.

Later, when Jesus was teaching Torah—good rabbi that he was—he invariably shocked his listeners, ratcheting up the expectations of God on those who seek to truly follow him. He said, for example: "You have heard how it was said, You shall not commit adultery. But I say this to you, if a man looks at a woman lustfully, he has already committed adultery with her in his heart" (Matt. 5:27–8). Seriously?! What was once a law of Moses, easy to track in one's life, just got a whole lot tougher. Who would even know if one was observing a law such as this? The religious leaders of the day thought he was nuts.

Jesus was a holy fool in his not worrying about the outcome or result of his teaching. Most important of all, he was a holy fool for allowing himself to be misunderstood, and later, mocked. He didn't defend himself when the meaning and purpose of his life was questioned by Pontius Pilate. He was willing to stand physically humiliated before crowds. In these ways alone, without any other agenda, there have been saints throughout history who have sought to imitate our foolish Lord.

I give you the end of a golden string;
Only wind it into a ball,
It will lead you in at Heaven's gate,
Built in Jerusalem's wall.
—William Blake, from *Jerusalem: The Emanation of the Giant Albion*

There is a perfect line, an uncut thread, "a golden string" throughout history that connects the foolishness of Christ with holy fools who have lived in every generation since his death and resurrection. They all have understood how being reviled can be a sign of blessedness or holiness, a true mark of God's Spirit alive inside of someone. When people witnessed this foolishness in Francis of Assisi eight hundred years ago, they called him *pazzo*. That's Italian for "crazy"—so, I guess, we can't avoid the term! The adjective, however, made Francis happy, in the sense that he knew: if they call you crazy or a fool, you must be doing something right!

The first instances of the crazy foolishness in Francis were outpourings of the Spirit in him. In other words, they are difficult to explain if you use only rational or pragmatic ways of understanding: Like when he stripped naked in front of a crowd in order to give everything back to his father that was rightfully his. Or when he began preaching to birds after people didn't seem to pay much heed to his words. Or when he scolded some of those birds for not listening carefully enough and chirping too loudly during Mass. Or when he joined a friend and disciple in deliberately humiliating himself—Francis had punished his friend by holy obedience (he was, by then, the friend's religious superior) for refusing to preach the Good News. The punishment was: go and preach, then, in your underwear. But a few minutes later, Francis chastised himself for being too severe— and decided to repent by stripping down to his breeches himself and joining the friend in the pulpit.

Why would someone do these things? They don't exactly make sense, do they? And yet, somehow, they did, and do.

Here's another bit of context: At the time that Francis and Brother Juniper, one of his closest friends and first followers, were becoming fools for Christ, there were professional fools—hired in noble and royal courts, as well as traveling from town to town—acting as entertainers but also as truth-tellers. They were often regarded as possessing a strange sort of wisdom that comes from being detached from the normal ways of the world. They never stopped reminding their audiences that the world will lie to you, deceive you with false appearances; that it may seem rational but actually it is mad. You see such a troupe in Shakespeare's *Hamlet*, for instance (act 5, scene 1). They are the grave diggers who appear after Ophelia's suicide, bantering about death, love, and the meaning of life.

However, such fools were often thought untrustworthy, since their profession was to trick people and play parts in a play. Many ordinary people were hesitant to trust Francis and the first Franciscans, too, linking them with this sort of fool. One early text reads, "Someone among them remarked: 'I wouldn't care to invite them into my house; they would probably steal my belongings.' And because of this, any number of insults were inflicted on them in many places. Therefore they very frequently sought lodging in the porticos of churches or houses."

But it was often the hired fool, dressed in motley silliness, juggling and telling stories, who was allowed to make jokes at the expense of the mighty. A common man or woman might not dare to say things that a fool could say with impunity. A fool was one who flouted conventions, poked fun at niceties, and got away with it because he was feebleminded (either pretending, or in reality). They were often regarded as medieval prophets who were able to see or understand things that others could not. Francis and Juniper appreciated these fools and emulated them when they became, as Francis himself put it, "Jugglers for God."

The most famous fool in history is a literary one rather than a religious one. His name is Don Quixote, and of course he is a fictional character drawn in the imagination of sixteenth-century Spanish novelist Miguel Cervantes. There is perhaps no better example of holy foolery than the ways in which Don Quixote acts as a knight errant, or "wandering knight," in an era when knighthood has all but vanished. He is a champion of chivalry, and chivalry is symbolic of virtue—both values of the past. So when Quixote prepares for battles and saves ladies in distress, we don't quite know whether he does it because he is mad, or because he refuses to be mad like the rest of the world that no longer does such things. And when he does things like tilt at windmills (imagining that they are giants), he seems to be really tipping the scales away from sanity. Yet, the paradox of *Don Quixote* remains—one never knows if its main character is a fool on purpose or by accident, and whether he is, ultimately, saner than all the rest of his contemporaries.

When Cervantes writes this of Don Quixote it is clear that his fool is also somehow heroic: "The truth is that when his mind was completely gone, he had the strangest thought any lunatic in the world ever had, which was that it seemed reasonable and necessary to him, both for the sake of his honor and as a service to the nation, to become a knight errant and travel the world with his armor and his horse to seek adventures and engage in everything he had read that knights errant engaged in, righting all manner of wrongs and, by seizing the opportunity and placing himself in danger and ending those wrongs, winning eternal renown and everlasting fame."

The first Franciscan friars were just as foolish as that. I even wonder if Cervantes had friars in mind when he created Don Quixote. You only have to replace a few words in those lines just quoted to see what I mean. Francis might almost be Don Quixote:

> The truth is that when his mind was completely gone, FRANCIS had the strangest thought any lunatic in the world ever had, which was that it seemed reasonable and necessary to him, both for the sake of his honor and as a service to the WORLD, to become a FRIAR and travel the world with his POVERTY and his RULE to seek adventures and engage in everything he had read that SAINTS engaged in, righting all manner of wrongs and, by seizing the opportunity and placing himself in danger and ending those wrongs, winning eternal renown and everlasting fame.

Men like Francis and Juniper take the Gospel seriously when it asks Christ-followers to "not store up treasures for yourselves on earth, where moth and woodworm destroy them and thieves can break in and steal. But store up treasures for yourselves in heaven, where neither moth nor woodworm destroys them and thieves cannot break in and steal. For wherever your treasure is, there will your heart be too. The lamp of the body is the eye. It follows that if your eye is clear, your whole body will be filled with light" (Matt. 6:19–22). Or, as one sees in the stories from the start of Francis's and Juniper's converted lives, when they follow Jesus just as the first disciples were told to do: "Take nothing for your journey, no staff, nor bag, nor bread, nor money—not even an extra tunic" (Lk. 9:3). These became essential teachings in their rule of life.

FOOLS KNOW THE TRUTH

The trouble with the world (majority opinion and societal expectations) as it is, isn't that the world is bad, but that we allow it to tell us who we ought to be. The Gospel is alternative, not mainstream. Remember the Beatitudes? How many people do you know who go seeking meekness, hunger, and peace instead of power? But if we want to follow Jesus, those are the values we'll uphold. And we won't uphold them by being "normal" in this world that is committed to things as they are.

Those who know the truth sometimes have to be foolish in order to communicate it. This is why the prophet Isaiah walked naked and barefoot for years (Isaiah 20), why the prophet Hosea married a harlot in order to make a point about faithfulness (Hosea 1), and why Jeremiah smashed a clay pot— because God told him to forcefully make a point

(Jeremiah 19). These are examples of being foolish in order to capture attention—or to subvert established authority. Neither Isaiah nor Hosea cared a wit about their reputations; they cared, instead, about changing minds.

They also understood that there is a mystery that explains life—and that mystery is never fully grasped through reason alone. Knowing the truth ultimately involves a kind of "letting go" of the way that our brain seeks to control our small world. Again, to quote G. K. Chesterton's *Orthodoxy* (the chapter "The Maniac" is required reading for all fools), "The whole secret of mysticism is this: that we can understand everything by the help of what we do not understand." The holy fool can see more, can understand more, can grasp her connection to a world that is endless, but only by accepting its mystery. This time, to paraphrase Chesterton, the fool is sane because he's able to float easily in an infinite sea, whereas reason seeks to cross the infinite sea and to make it finite.

When being a fool involves humiliation, a holy fool doesn't mind that either. As the Spanish writer Miguel de Unamuno wrote in his journal when he was realizing that learning was not the way to God, "One must seek for the truth of things, not their reason, and truth is sought in humility." Perhaps only a Christian would be able to appreciate this fully, since Christians have as their prime example a God who emptied and then further humbled himself.

Even so, other traditions have holy fools too. Hindu religious men in India often leave behind careers late in life to become what is called a *sadhu*, devoted to asceticism and wandering. The young look to them as spiritual teachers. In Buddhism, holy lunacy often exhibits itself in laughter—deep, belly laughter! The notion is that only the person who has abandoned worldly cares and drunk deeply in the spiritual life is able to laugh in such a genuine way. The Laughing Buddha of Buddhist lore goes from town to town spreading joy and happiness.

Not so for Francis. He didn't like laughter because in the milieu of late medieval Europe, laughter closely resembled frivolity. *A Mirror of Perfection*, an early account of Francis's life and teachings, tells of him teaching the importance of being joyful, but then adding that he wouldn't want "this joy to be shown through laughter or even empty words. . . . [H]e abhorred laughter and an idle word to an exceptional degree. . . . By a joyful face he understood the fervor and solicitude, the disposition and readiness of a mind and body to willingly undertake every good work." At its root, this shows that Christian holy foolery has always had an important purpose.

We can't get away from the fact that our inspiration comes first and foremost from the example of Jesus during his Passion. He was willingly mocked and humiliated on his way to the cross. He could have arranged things differently. Why did he allow the stripping off of his clothes, the scourging, being made fun of by the Roman soldiers, and the jeering of the crowds? He was a fool to make a point about humility. In the process, he demonstrated how like us he is. We easily feel foolish, and spend so much time trying to avoid the experience. This is why a holy fool is taught, today, to actually seek out humiliating moments as a kind of exercise, in order to teach us the kind of wisdom that comes only from overcoming the all-too-present self. (See, for example, the stories "When Juniper Went Naked to Town," and "Why Juniper Played on a Seesaw in Rome" in chapter 5.) Today, this is the rarest kind of Christian foolery, and a type of spiritual practice that I hope may be revived at least a bit with the encouragement found in this book.

The purpose of *St. Francis Holy Fool Prayer Book* is to encourage us to be fools for Christ and provide some resources by which to do it. Let our words and actions run counter to what society expects, because in so doing, we might be most faithfully living the Gospel.

You'll encounter plenty of Scripture to keep you focused, some of which I've already mentioned. There are passages from the Gospels, the prophets of the Hebrew Bible, and from St. Paul, who wrote a lot in defense of foolishness in one of his most popular letters, 1 Corinthians. You will encounter these teachings in the week's worth of prayer and in the inspiration, "Seven Themes for Seven Days."

As you go, now, keep in mind that, for people like Francis and Juniper, being a holy fool is often not just a way of discipleship but an act of protest. They wanted people to see the truth, and sometimes we wear such thick blinders that we need to be shocked in order to see through them. Being a fool can be a way of finding a new source of confidence, apart from what the world offers and values, in priorities that are known primarily to others who share in the foolishness. Kahlil Gibran expresses this in an early work when he writes, "I have found both freedom and safety in my madness; the freedom of loneliness and the safety from being understood, for those who understand us enslave something in us." May this book, in some small measure, set you free.

I
INSPIRATION
LOOKING TO ST. FRANCIS AND BROTHER JUNIPER

Then he entered into the city of Assisi and began, as though drunk with the Holy Spirit, to praise God aloud in the streets and the squares." That is how the first-ever biography of Francis relays one of the saint's earliest public expressions of faith. The author who wrote that account, Thomas of Celano, knew Francis personally. The analogy to drunkenness—public drunkenness, no less!—was clearly deliberate. That's what many thought of Francis in those early days.

He wasn't drunk on alcohol, of course. But to extend the metaphor: he was tipsy, light-headed, even to the extent of being louder in public than is usually deemed appropriate. He wasn't acting like he was drunk; he was praising God aloud "as though drunk." There's a difference.

A holy fool *does* sometimes act a part. He will pretend to be something that he isn't in order to make a point, or to get a message across. For example, this is what Brother Bernard did only a few years later, when he went to Bologna and sat in the piazza all day, for days on end, looking like what soon came to be known as a Franciscan fool: unshaven, filthy, patches on his clothing, an incongruous smile on his face. "Who are you? Why are you here?" someone finally asked Bernard. Which is when he pulled from his pocket the radically simple rule of life that he and the first Franciscans lived by, and shared it with them. Within days there were novice friars in Bologna.

Brother Juniper did the same thing, over and over—allowing himself to be poked fun of, even deliberately humiliating himself, in order to express the spirit of his faith and commitments. There was the time, for instance, when Juniper wanted to make himself a laughingstock before others and stripped himself of all but his underwear (yes, this is something of a recurring theme!), and carried a bundle of his habit and other clothes into the city of Viterbo—half-naked, right into the marketplace. This story is told in full in chapter 5. Many youths came by and believed that Juniper had lost his senses. They threw stones and mud at him and pushed him around, spitting words of insult. But Juniper stayed there most of that day, enduring it happily. As the day was coming to a close, he then went to sleep at the convent nearby.

When the other friars saw what he'd done, they were angry. One said, "Let's lock him up." Another, "He deserves worse that that!" And another, "He's caused a scandal to the whole Order." But Juniper with joy answered, "I deserve all these punishments, and far worse." Such a response surely made the others pause.

But before this contrived foolery could take place, there was the unpretending kind—the drunk with the Spirit kind:

> It was in the days when Francis was still wearing his secular clothing, even though he had begun to renounce the things of the world.

4

He had been going around Assisi looking mortified and unkempt, wearing his penance in his appearance in such a way that people thought he had become a fool. He was mocked and laughed at, and pelted with stones and mud by both those who knew him and those who did not. But Francis endured these things with patience and joy, as if he did not hear the taunts at all and had no means of responding to them.

Somewhere between these two kinds of prayerful foolishness comes the ability to laugh at the world when it places value on what is really without meaning.

St. Francis wasn't always a saint or a holy fool. Quite the opposite, in fact.

In this description of Francis before his conversion began, Thomas of Celano didn't mean the last part as praise: "Almost up to the twenty-fifth year of his age, he squandered and wasted his time miserably. Indeed, he outdid all his contemporaries in vanities and he came to be a promoter of evil and was more abundantly zealous for all kinds of foolishness." But it was soon after his twenty-fifth year that God took hold of Francis's life and Francis began to seek more important things.

Quickly, in a matter of a few years, Francis and the first friends who joined him in the new charism that came to be called Franciscan—men like Brother Bernard and Brother Juniper—came to represent the most important moment for holy foolishness in the history of the Christian West. Together they created a renaissance of this unique way of living and communicating the Gospel. Through them, faith was invigorated with innocence and simplicity. Clericalism, dogmatism, and crusading had dominated the Church for centuries, but soon gave way and were transformed.

Other religious orders at that time were focusing on theological teaching and doctrinal preaching. Francis, Juniper, and the others had a different sort of mission. They wanted to be, for lack of a better word, simple.

Innocence is vastly underrated today. Francis possessed it without even knowing that he did. That's of course the whole idea. I can't read these lines from *Don Quixote* without thinking again of the earnest young Francis: "His armor being now furbished, his helmet made perfect, his horse and himself provided with names, he found nothing wanting but a lady to be in love with." Cervantes is referring to his knight-errant hero, but it might as well again be Francis, who walked just as boldly and foolishly on the uncertain path that was his early conversion. For Francis, that lady soon became "Lady Poverty," to whom he quixotically devoted his entire life and then told his friends all about it.

"What woman are you thinking about, Francis?" his old friends asked him one day, expecting the daydreaming or vain friend of their youth to answer. He shocked them when he replied:

> "You are right! I was thinking about taking a wife more noble, wealthier, and more beautiful than you have ever seen." They laughed at him. For he said this not of his own accord, but because he was inspired by God. In fact, the bride was the true religion that he later embraced, a bride more noble, richer and more beautiful because of her poverty.

It was early on that Juniper joined Francis, and Juniper possessed a kind of innocence that might even have been greater than the founder's. It often seemed that Juniper could see nothing but the ideals and goals of Christian life. Charity, for instance, led him to forget himself, and he was often rebuked, even by Francis, for running around without clothes on, since he'd given them all away. Humility was so much his focus that he often appeared ridiculous before others, to the point that his brother friars were embarrassed about him, as we've seen. "I wish that I had a whole forest of such Junipers!" Francis once punned, when confronted with this, clearly taking the opposite view.

Like all the holy fools in Christian history, both Francis and Juniper were possessed with a different way of looking at the world. They were influenced by the Holy Spirit in such a way that one might say they actually saw a different world from other people. Pouring rain, for instance, not only didn't deter Francis when he was walking one day with Brother Leo, another early friend and companion, on the road, but became something that he genuinely (and annoyingly, to Leo!) wanted to experience fresh and anew. With a similar conversion of the senses, Francis once praised Juniper, who was cooking for his brother friars, for his ability to turn garlic into lavender. Contemporary Franciscan Fr. Murray Bodo has recently imagined Juniper's response to this as, "I never thought of it before, but it is true. I often used to smell lavender when the brothers would bring home scraps they had begged." Most anyone else would have smelled something else entirely.

They were foolish in another important respect, as well. They lived without certainties that most people take for granted. This is because they wanted to follow their Savior who said, "Foxes have holes and the birds of the air have nests, but the Son of man has nowhere to lay his head" (Lk. 9:58). So Francis and Juniper didn't want homes or a secure future or even roofs over their heads. This is how holy foolishness can sometimes involve seeking "the peace of wild things," as it was recently stated by the poet and farmer Wendell Berry.

Unpredictability becomes a virtue for the Franciscan holy fool, since there is a grace and freedom in the created, wild world that human-made institutions and structures just can't quite match. "O Lord, how manifold are your works! in wisdom you have made them all; the earth is full of your creatures," as the psalmist says (Ps. 104:25). In fact, pausing to notice or enjoy these things becomes more foolish all the time. Just imagine the man who talks to animals as if they were his brothers and sisters, or a woman who gathers wild, free-ranging dandelions and values them as the loveliest of flowers of spring. Francis of Assisi threw himself in the snow, preached to birds, walked carefully over stones, and refused most everyday comforts. He was probably the freest man the world has ever known.

The Sufi poet Rumi once told a story of a man who was confronted by a police officer. The cop believed he was drunk. The man was asleep, leaning up against a wall in town when the officer approached and asked what he'd been drinking. "Whatever was in this bottle," the man responded. "What was that, exactly?" said the cop. "That which now fills me," said the accused. "Come on!" exclaims the officer, becoming upset. The officer was, Rumi used to explain, "like a donkey stuck in the mud." "You can't see what intoxicates me," the man finally replied. That's the holy in holy foolery. "And if I were still unhappy and reasoning perfectly, I'd be sitting upright and lecturing with the sheikhs," he added. That's the foolery—and how its wisdom penetrates the cloudiness of everyday life.

For eight hundred years there has been a way of prayer that's deeply rooted in the teachings of Christ but practiced mostly outside the walls of a church. To practice one's faith with foolishness in the ways that are particularly Franciscan is a spiritual gift (not so much a practice, but a gift.) It didn't originate with the life and teachings of Francis of Assisi and Brother Juniper—holy fools trace their spiritual practice at least back to Christ—but it was galvanized in their unique lives, in their particular time and place.

They discovered a life of joy, simplicity, and wonder. Their gift for expressing God's joy and love involved being small not strong, avoiding positions of power altogether, thinking not about results but about virtue, and enjoying rather than avoiding moments of insecurity, fear, and awkwardness. These practices for being foolish in the eyes of the world were, for them, a sure way to discover the presence of God. That is what is available to anyone who chooses to walk the path of the Gospel in these countercultural ways.

Don't get me wrong: The holy fool's way is too radical for most people. It is for the few, not the many. When the famous Renaissance monk Erasmus wrote his satirical *In Praise of Folly*, he didn't recommend anything like what Francis, Juniper, and their friends lived out. By Erasmus's time, there was no one more arrogant in the Church than the mendicant orders, including the Franciscans, and they had largely exchanged their founding values and spiritual practices for others that were more in keeping with the values of the world. Erasmus ripped them apart, exposing their hypocrisies.

A holy fool's ways also aren't easy. But in their foolishness, Francis and Juniper remind anyone of what is the heart and soul of Jesus's teaching. You can't learn the Gospel simply in books. You have to put these things into practice. But I think you will find, maybe to your great surprise, that this foolish way makes great sense, especially today, as a corrective to what we know as twenty-first-century Christianity.

II
How Fools Might Pray
—AT LEAST FOR A WEEK

A holy fool prays, probably more than most people, because she knows how much she is in need of what prayer accomplishes.

There is very little by way of speculative theology in fools' prayer. That's not the purpose of it. Instead, prayer is for praise, relationship, gratitude, even celebrating the paradoxes and mysteries of faith. Prayer is for thanking God and aligning the heart more with God's desires.

Mornings and evenings are good times to pray, or to practice praying—the two can be one and the same. Both mornings and evenings are times to mark the beginning of what is new. In the morning, these lines from William Blake (which also beautifully recall how heaven and earth are inextricably linked) are worth remembering:

> Awake the dawn that sleeps in heaven; let light
> Rise from the chambers of the east, and bring
> The honied dew that cometh on waking day.

There are fresh possibilities as we thank God for eyes and hearts that open with the rising sun. The day has come around again.

Evenings are different. Each evening we have the emotions of the day and usually the exhaustion, too, to bring to a close. We do this with remembering praise and by expressing desires for the morrow. We also recall what has just happened; perhaps we ask forgiveness for what we've done or not done. And often we ask, with saints throughout the centuries, for the Lord to protect us through the silent hours of the night.

This is what we'll do for a practice week.

WHAT TO EXPECT EACH DAY

The sequence for each day of this special morning and evening liturgy is as follows:

A. PREPARATION (a very simple prayer of intention)

B. THE WORD OF GOD—usually a Gospel sentence or other line from the New Testament that is pungent with the theme of the day. The same one is used for both morning and evening each day. The brevity of these passages can be profound—and encourage memorization.

C. SILENCE (more than a moment; take a minute or more if you can)

D. SONG OF MY SOUL (the psalm selection)

E. A READING FROM THE PROPHETS (a canticle from the Hebrew prophets)

F. NEW TESTAMENT READING

G. SILENCE (again)

H. AN EARLY FRANCISCAN SAYING

I. A SPIRITUAL PRACTICE (this is where the praying turns into action)

There are many ways that you may choose to use these morning and evening prayers in your life. They can function as a special energizer of prayer in your devotional life. Prayer needs sparks in order to keep firing. As you walk along with Francis and Juniper and pray the themes that formed their spiritual lives, you will reinvigorate your own.

First, if you already have a prayer book you use daily, there are ways to pray this book as a supplement to your usual practice. Perhaps you wish to focus your prayer time with Francis and Juniper on a special weekend or a weeklong spiritual retreat on holy foolery or a broader Franciscan theme.

The divine hours of prayer have, from their earliest beginnings in the ancient synagogue, been intended for group use; so, you may wish, in addition, to pray these short liturgies together with others in a group devoted to learning more about Francis of Assisi, Brother Juniper, and the charism of early Franciscanism. Otherwise, as you pray alone, know that you are not alone. You join with thous-ands of others around the world both past and present who have prayed similar words, as well. For them and for us, daily prayer is a means of beginning anew each day.

Second, if you already have a prayer practice and a prayer book, this book's offering of a week of prayers may be a temporary substitute for your regular prayer practice. You may wish to make a special prayer week, finding some fresh inspiration by praying, exploring, and living into the themes of the holy fool. It is natural to come to these points in any prayer life, when something new is needed, and that explains the necessity of works such as this one.

Third, while I hope that these prayers become a personal and daily prayer book for many, it may also appeal to those who may wish to pray in community, in study groups, or even academic settings. There is no way to really understand the "poor followers" of Christ, as Francis and Juniper referred to themselves, without enjoining their spiritual lives, its themes, and the very words of their prayers.

SEVEN THEMES FOR SEVEN DAYS

We will begin with seven themes—one per day— that emerge from the life and writings of and about St. Francis and Brother Juniper. These themes will provide a framework and subject for each of our seven days of prayer.

Day One—There Is Wisdom in Foolishness (Sunday)
Again, to quote William Blake (he was a holy fool), "If the fool would persist in his folly, he would become wise." In other words, as in every aspect of the Christian life, there is *telos* to what we do and who we are. Telos is a Greek word used by Aristotle as well as by St. Paul. It means purpose, goal. Know this right here and now before you go any further: fools are fools not only because it is the way to follow Christ, but because it is the way to truth. The world can see a holy fool only as a tragic figure, crushed despite his goodness, but we know differently. The fool's way is the way to a blessed

future as he or she is slowly becoming what has been promised and what we yearn for:

> In days to come the mountain of the Lord's house shall be established as the highest of the mountains, and shall be raised above the hills; all the nations shall stream to it. Many peoples shall come and say, "Come, let us go up to the mountain of the Lord, to the house of the God of Jacob; that he may teach us his ways and that we may walk in his paths." For out of Zion shall go forth instruction, and the word of the Lord from Jerusalem. He shall judge between the nations, and shall arbitrate for many peoples; they shall beat their swords into ploughshares, and their spears into pruning-hooks; nation shall not lift up sword against nation, neither shall they learn war any more (Isa. 2:2–4).

Day Two—There Is Strength in Powerlessness (Monday)

Essential to any spiritual practice of holy foolishness is acknowledging that the only lasting power and strength in the world and in our lives rests in God—the God who came as a baby in a manger. Is there any greater example of powerlessness than the human infant? Of all the ways for God to enter the world, that is the one God chose, demonstrating the theme for this day: there is strength in powerlessness. The theme is emphasized in the readings from the Gospels, showing that there is no greater holy fool than Jesus himself, and that there are reasons why– not just the birth of Jesus, but his Passion, too–that provide the ultimate example for our lives.

Day Three—There Is Joy in Forgiveness (Tuesday)

Holy foolishness cannot exist without a profound and radical sense of forgiveness in our lives—a true "letting go." This becomes a sense of relief that is sometimes powerfully experienced with tears and dancing and shouting when you repent of your sins. As one contemporary author who studied holy fools has cleverly put it, "As I continued to meet holy fools, I noticed that they viewed repentance as the essential curriculum for spiritual kindergarten, college, and postdoctoral studies." Allow yourself to be open to experiences and emotions such as these on day three; they are familiar to holy fools of all Christian traditions. As St. Antony of Egypt once said: "Here comes the time when people will behave like madmen, and if they see anybody who does not behave like that, they will rebel against him and say: 'You are mad'—because he is not like them."

Day Four—The Humble Are Blessed (Wednesday)

In the Gospels, several of the Beatitudes are teachings of Jesus that we don't—*can we admit this?*—readily or easily believe. I'm talking about "blessed are the meek," etc. We think of them as somewhat irrelevant to daily life in the real world, or as something for a future age when the world has changed from what it is. But when St. Paul says, "The message of the Cross is folly for those who are on the way to ruin, but for those of us who are on the road to salvation it is the power of God" (1 Cor. 1:18), he's making a point about what is real. It turns out that much of that "real world" stuff that we've been told we should preoccupy ourselves with, is not, in fact, real at all. This is a day to pray on this theme, and seek to create in our lives the absence of vanity and egotism that otherwise fills most of everyday life around us.

Day Five—The Pure in Heart Are Blessed (Thursday)

This day is all about treasuring what is foolish because now we accept and realize that the fool is one who has come to see life as it really is. A fool is able to live life to the fullest because of what she understands, and who she is becoming. No longer is human existence all about surviving or competition, we realize. The philosopher Friedrich Nietzsche grew to hate Christianity and what it taught when he fashioned ideas of the superman and will to power. He couldn't stand the Christian's willingness to be weak. He found it pitiable, not something to be imitated. But Nietzsche was wrong. The saints are right. As the Bible says,

Christ "emptied himself" (Phil. 2:7) for our sake. That's our model, and that's what we try to do, in following him.

Along the way, we avoid self-delusion and chasing after things (stuff, people, love, reputation, fame)—these efforts that fill the will-to-have, will-to-be, and any other process by which people are taught to self-fulfill. The holy fool knows life more simply, closer to its real essence, and, as a result, more beautifully. One contemporary author sums this up nicely when she imagines the people who don't get it: "How foolish to be an unholy fool!"

Day Six—Folly Is Another Name for Righteousness (Friday)

Why is this theme essential? Because spiritual practice is never something we do just for us, in the quiet of our house or room. Our lives are inextricably intertwined with the lives of others anyway, but we also are supposed to deliberately connect them, and help each other. Even (or especially!) holy foolishness can help the people around us.

Why is folly another name for righteousness? Because it is foolish in the eyes of the world to do what brings us no earthly reward. It is crazy to spend time and focus energy on what brings us no glory. That's because the world assigns meaning to what the holy fool knows is without meaning. This is when what we do begins to resemble art—with unexpected revelations of beauty, new perceptions of what's real. As Thomas Merton once appreciated in the playwright Eugene Ionesco, "If one does not understand the usefulness of the useless and the uselessness of the useful, one cannot understand art." And as St. Paul once said: "Since in the wisdom of God the world was unable to recognize God through wisdom, it was God's own pleasure to save believers through the folly of the gospel" (1 Cor. 1:21).

Day Seven—True Wisdom Brings Peace and Justice (Saturday)

This is a tough one, and that's why it comes last. It is difficult because a holy fool tries never to be self-righteous. Concerns for self undermine anything else that a holy fool might do. Still, a holy fool is often a kind of prophet, and deliberately so—so the line is a narrow one to walk. As you grow in wisdom, remember the book of Wisdom and how the people complain about the "righteous man": "Let us lie in wait for the righteous man, because he is inconvenient to us and opposes our actions; he reproaches us for sins against the law, and accuses us of sins against our training. He professes to have knowledge of God, and calls himself a child of the Lord" (Wisd. 2:12). The righteous one is not wrong—doing what is right even when it's uncomfortable is the epitome of holy foolishness. We have to remember who we are serving. Also, a holy fool knows the truth of what poet Wendell Berry has recently said: "A change of heart or of values without a practice is only another pointless luxury of a passively consumptive way of life."

III
DAILY
OFFICE

for HOLY FOOLS

SUNDAY

Theme/Intent: There Is Wisdom in Foolishness

PREPARATION

Heavenly Father, I am your child,
That I know, not because we are alike,
But because in the morning I look to You.
In my sometimes feeble, fumbling ways.
You are all I seek. Amen.

THE WORD OF GOD

Here we are, fools for Christ's sake. (1 Cor. 4:10)

Silence

Song of My Soul (Psalm 19)

The heavens declare the glory of God,
    and the firmament shows his handiwork.
One day tells its tale to another,
    and one night imparts knowledge to another.
Although they have no words or language,
    and their voices are not heard,
Their sound has gone out into all lands,
    and their message to the ends of the world.
In the deep has he set a pavilion for the sun;
    it comes forth like a bridegroom out of his chamber;
    it rejoices like a champion to run its course.
It goes forth from the uttermost edge of the heavens
and runs about to the end of it again;
    nothing is hidden from its burning heat.

The law of the Lord is perfect and revives the soul;
   the testimony of the Lord is sure
and gives wisdom to the innocent.
The statutes of the Lord are just and rejoice the
   heart;
   the commandment of the Lord is clear
and gives light to the eyes.
The fear of the Lord is clean and endures for ever;
   the judgments of the Lord are true
and righteous altogether.
More to be desired are they than gold,
more than much fine gold,
sweeter far than honey, than honey in the comb.
(vs. 1–10)

A READING FROM THE PROPHETS

The days of punishment have come, the days of recompense have come; Israel cries, "The prophet is a fool, the man of the spirit is mad!" . . . The prophet is a sentinel for my God. (Hos. 9:7–8a)

NEW TESTAMENT READING

For it seems to me that God has put us apostles on show right at the end, like men condemned to death: we have been exhibited as a spectacle to the whole universe, both angelic and human. Here we are, fools for Christ's sake, while you are the clever ones in Christ; we are weak, while you are strong; you are honored, while we are disgraced. To this day, we go short of food and drink and clothes, we are beaten up and we have no homes; we earn our living by laboring with our own hands; when we are cursed, we answer with a blessing; when we are hounded, we endure it passively; when we are insulted, we give a courteous answer. We are treated even now as the dregs of the world, the very lowest scum (1 Cor. 4:9–13).

Silence

AN EARLY FRANCISCAN SAYING
Blessed is the one who knows how to keep and hide the revelations of God, for there is nothing hidden that God may not reveal when it pleases him.
—Brother Giles of Assisi

A SPIRITUAL PRACTICE
Today, alone, somewhere outdoors, try preaching to the birds. If it happens to be winter and there are no birds to be found where you are, preach to the squirrels. Begin by speaking silently, if you prefer, in your mind. But stand before them and express yourself from your heart. Record how it felt. Do it again tomorrow.

EVENING PRAYER
SUNDAY
Theme/Intent: There Is Wisdom in Foolishness

PREPARATION
Holy One, I am following
In your path.
When I don't understand what's next,
I am comforted to know that
You do.

THE WORD OF GOD
Here we are, fools for Christ's sake. (1 Cor. 4:10)

Silence

Song of My Soul (Psalm 16)
I will bless the LORD who gives me counsel;
    my heart teaches me, night after night.
I have set the LORD always before me;
    because he is at my right hand I shall not fall.
My heart, therefore, is glad, and my spirit rejoices;
    my body also shall rest in hope.
For you will not abandon me to the grave,
    nor let your holy one see the Pit.
You will show me the path of life;
    in your presence there is fullness of joy,
    and in your right hand are pleasures for ever-
    more.
(vs. 7–11)

A READING FROM THE PROPHETS

Thus says the LORD, your Redeemer, who formed you in the womb: I am the LORD, who made all things, who alone stretched out the heavens . . . who frustrates the omens of liars . . . who turns back the wise . . . confirms the word of his servant, and fulfills the prediction of his messengers.
(Isa. 44:24–25)

NEW TESTAMENT READING

Jesus said, "Do not store up treasures for yourselves on earth, where moth and woodworm destroy them and thieves can break in and steal. But store up treasures for yourselves in heaven, where neither moth nor woodworm destroys them and thieves cannot break in and steal. For wherever your treasure is, there will your heart be too. The lamp of the body is the eye. It follows that if your eye is clear, your whole body will be filled with light."
(Matt. 6:19–22)

Silence

AN EARLY FRANCISCAN SAYING

As you announce peace with your mouth, make sure that greater peace is in your hearts. Let no one be provoked to anger or scandal through you, but may everyone be drawn to peace, kindness, and harmony through your gentleness. For we have been called to this: to heal the wounded, bind up the broken, and recall the erring. —Francis of Assisi

A SPIRITUAL PRACTICE

Are there decisions you make in your life based in your faith that cause you to seem somewhat foolish compared to others? If not, perhaps there should be. If there are, rather than telling others about them like a prophet might feel compelled to do, do you hold them silently? Others probably still notice. A fool rarely is hidden for long.

MONDAY

Theme/Intent: There Is Strength in Powerlessness

PREPARATION

Holy One, I am here with nothing.
I am like a bird aloft, with only
You holding up my wings.
Keep Your air under me today,
please.

THE WORD OF GOD

For the wisdom of the world is folly to God.
(1 Cor. 3:19)

Silence

Song of My Soul (Psalm 57)

Be merciful to me, O God, be merciful,
for I have taken refuge in you;
> in the shadow of your wings will I take refuge
> until this time of trouble has gone by.
I will call upon the Most High God,
> the God who maintains my cause.
He will send from heaven and save me;
he will confound those who trample upon me;
> God will send forth his love and his faithfulness.
I lie in the midst of lions that devour the people;
> their teeth are spears and arrows,
> their tongue a sharp sword.

They have laid a net for my feet,
and I am bowed low; they have dug a pit before me,
  but have fallen into it themselves.
Exalt yourself above the heavens, O God,
  and your glory over all the earth. (vs. 1–6)

A READING FROM THE PROPHETS

Hear the word of the LORD, O nations, and declare
it in the coastlands far away; say, "He who scattered
Israel will gather him, and will keep him as a
shepherd a flock."

For the LORD has ransomed Jacob, and has
redeemed him from hands too strong for him.
(Jer. 31:10–11)

NEW TESTAMENT READING

Pilate then had Jesus taken away and scourged; and
after this, the soldiers twisted some thorns into a
crown and put it on his head and dressed him in
a purple robe. They kept coming up to him and
saying, "Hail, king of the Jews!" and slapping him
in the face. Pilate came outside again and said to
them, "Look, I am going to bring him out to you
to let you see that I find no case against him." Jesus
then came out wearing the crown of thorns and the
purple robe. Pilate said, "Here is the man."
(John 19:1–5)

Silence

AN EARLY FRANCISCAN SAYING

The sisters shall not acquire anything as their own, neither a house nor a place nor anything at all; instead, as pilgrims and strangers in this world who serve the Lord in poverty and humility. . . . Nor should they feel ashamed, since the Lord made Himself poor for us in this world. This is that summit of highest poverty which has established you, my dearest sisters, as heirs and queens of the kingdom of heaven; it has made you poor in the things of this world but has exalted you in virtue.
—Clare of Assisi

A SPIRITUAL PRACTICE

It is so ingrained in us to "overcome" our adversaries, to "stand up for ourselves" and for what's right. That, of course, is not what Jesus did before Pilate, and only a holy fool would follow his example, even in that. Compose a short prayer today—it can be only one line long—speaking to God of your desire to be faithful even in this difficult way.

EVENING PRAYER

MONDAY

Theme/Intent: There Is Strength in Powerlessness

PREPARATION

Heavenly Father, I don't know where I'm going
or what I am necessarily supposed to do.
But I know that following you doesn't always
make sense, as I have learned what sense is.
So, I will listen with the ears of my heart.
Amen.

THE WORD OF GOD

For the wisdom of the world is folly to God.
(1 Cor. 3:19)

Silence

Song of My Soul (Psalm 57)

My heart is firmly fixed, O God, my heart is fixed;
    I will sing and make melody.
Wake up, my spirit; awake, lute and harp;
    I myself will waken the dawn.
I will confess you among the peoples, O LORD;
    I will sing praise to you among the nations.
For your lovingkindness is greater than the heavens,
    and your faithfulness reaches to the clouds.
Exalt yourself above the heavens, O God,
    and your glory over all the earth. (vs. 7–11)

A READING FROM THE PROPHETS

Then David blessed the LORD in the presence of all the assembly; David said: "Blessed are you, O Lord, the God of our ancestor Israel, forever and ever. Yours, O LORD, are the greatness, the power, the glory, the victory, and the majesty; for all that is in the heavens and on the earth is yours; yours is the kingdom, O LORD, and you are exalted as head above all. Riches and honor come from you, and you rule over all. In your hand are power and might; and it is in your hand to make great and to give strength to all. And now, our God, we give thanks to you and praise your glorious name. (1 Chr. 29:10–13)

NEW TESTAMENT READING

First thing in the morning, the chief priests, together with the elders and scribes and the rest of the Sanhedrin, had their plan ready. They had Jesus bound and took him away and handed him over to Pilate. Pilate put to him this question, "Are you the king of the Jews?" He replied, "It is you who say it." And the chief priests brought many accusations against him. Pilate questioned him again, "Have you no reply at all? See how many accusations they are bringing against you!" But, to Pilate's surprise, Jesus made no further reply. (Mk. 15:1–5)

Silence

AN EARLY FRANCISCAN SAYING

Brother Juniper once determined by himself to keep silence for a six-month period. He did it this way. The first month for the love of the Eternal Father. The second month for love of Jesus Christ his Son. The third month for love of the Holy Ghost. The fourth in reverence to the most holy Virgin Mary. And from then forward, he spent each day in silence in honor of one of the saints. So he passed six whole months without speaking.

—from *The Little Flowers of St. Francis*

A SPIRITUAL PRACTICE

How often do you defend yourself before others? The next time you feel slighted or misunderstood or worse, keep silent, being the fool that your Lord was before Pilate.

TUESDAY

Theme/Intent: There Is Joy in Forgiveness

PREPARATION

Father, Son, and Holy Spirit,
I need You today.
Reveal to me whatever is necessary.
Startle me. Surprise me!
Or just make it plain as day
where I need to forgive,
or be forgiven.

THE WORD OF GOD

Do not stifle the Spirit or despise the gift
of prophecy. (1 Thess. 5:19)

Silence

Song of My Soul (Psalm 30)

I will exalt you, O LORD,
because you have lifted me up
    and have not let my enemies triumph over me.
O LORD my God, I cried out to you,
    and you restored me to health.
You brought me up, O LORD, from the dead;
    you restored my life as I was going down to
    the grave.
Sing to the LORD, you servants of his;
    give thanks for the remembrance of his holiness.

For his wrath endures but the twinkling of an eye,
    his favor for a lifetime.
Weeping may spend the night,
    but joy comes in the morning. (vs. 1–6)

A READING FROM THE PROPHETS

Seek the LORD while he may be found, call upon him while he is near; let the wicked forsake their way, and the unrighteous their thoughts; let them return to the LORD, that he may have mercy on them, and to our God, for he will abundantly pardon. (Isa. 55:6–7)

NEW TESTAMENT READING

So [Jesus] told them this parable. "Which one of you with a hundred sheep, if he lost one, would fail to leave the ninety-nine in the desert and go after the missing one till he found it? And when he found it, would he not joyfully take it on his shoulders and then, when he got home, call together his friends and neighbors, saying to them, 'Rejoice with me, I have found my sheep that was lost.' In the same way, I tell you, there will be more rejoicing in heaven over one sinner repenting than over ninety-nine upright people who have no need of repentance."
(Lk. 15:3–7)

Silence

AN EARLY FRANCISCAN SAYING

The brothers should always be careful that, no matter where they are, whether in a hermitage or any other place, not to appropriate any place as their own, or even to possess it instead of another. And whoever may come to them, either friend or foe, even thief or robber, they should receive all with kindness. And no matter where they are, they should spiritually and diligently show reverence and honor toward one another without complaints. And they should always be careful not to appear sad and gloomy on the outside, like hypocrites do, but show themselves to be joyful, cheerful, and gracious to others, in the name of the Lord. —Francis of Assisi

A SPIRITUAL PRACTICE

Bring an unforgiven sin to God this morning. (Best of all, and if you are Catholic, take that sin to confession.) Or, perhaps there is a sin you've already confessed but still haven't resolved with another person or within yourself. Do what you need to do to bring it to its full conclusion today and this week—for God's sake, your sake, and to find the true joy of forgiveness.

EVENING PRAYER
TUESDAY
Theme/Intent: There Is Joy in Forgiveness

PREPARATION

Holy Spirit,
I'm tired at the end of a long day,
but I'm dancing inside,
knowing that no matter what happens,
or happened,
You were with me in it! Amen.

THE WORD OF GOD
Do not stifle the Spirit or despise the gift
of prophecy. (1 Thess. 5:19)

Silence

Song of My Soul (Psalm 30)

While I felt secure, I said, "I shall never be disturbed.
You, LORD, with your favor, made me as strong as
the mountains."
Then you hid your face, and I was filled with fear.
I cried to you, O LORD; I pleaded with the LORD,
saying,
"What profit is there in my blood, if I go down to
the Pit?
will the dust praise you or declare your faithfulness?
Hear, O LORD, and have mercy upon me;
O LORD, be my helper."
You have turned my wailing into dancing;

you have put off my sack-cloth and clothed
me with joy.
Therefore my heart sings to you without ceasing;
O Lord my God, I will give you thanks for
ever. (vs. 7–13)

A READING FROM THE PROPHETS

They shall come and sing aloud on the height of
Zion, and they shall be radiant over the goodness of
the Lord, over the grain, the wine, and the oil, and
. . . their life shall become like a watered garden, and
they shall never languish again. Then shall the young
women rejoice in the dance, and the young men and
the old shall be merry. I will turn their mourning
into joy, I will comfort them, and give them gladness
for sorrow . . . and my people shall be satisfied with
my bounty, says the Lord. (Jer. 31:12–14)

NEW TESTAMENT READING

Always be joyful, then, in the Lord; I repeat, be
joyful. Let your good sense be obvious to everybody.
The Lord is near. Never worry about anything; but
tell God all your desires of every kind in prayer and
petition shot through with gratitude, and the peace
of God which is beyond our understanding will guard
your hearts and your thoughts in Christ Jesus. Finally,
brothers, let your minds be filled with everything
that is true, everything that is honorable, everything
that is upright and pure, everything that we love and
admire—with whatever is good and praiseworthy.
(Phil. 4:4–8)

Silence

AN EARLY FRANCISCAN SAYING

Sinners will come back to their God by humility, not by scolding. Christ tells us that those who are well do not need a physician, but those who are sick do.

—Francis of Assisi

A SPIRITUAL PRACTICE

Some of us are simply not good at allowing joy to fill us. (I count myself in this camp, much of the time.) Perhaps we were taught to be more circumspect, not to easily show our feelings. For a few minutes, as long as you are able, stretch your arms wide and hold your palms facing out as if you might catch a huge beach ball that's about to be thrown your direction. Close your eyes. Then, catch it!

WEDNESDAY
Theme/Intent: Blessed Are the Humble

PREPARATION

Holy, Happy One!
I don't often think of You that way—
Holy and Happy.
But I hear Your song in the morning
and I want to sing it with You,
today. Amen.

THE WORD OF GOD

Jesus said to them, "In truth I tell you, tax collectors
and prostitutes are making their way into the
kingdom of God before you." (Matt. 21:31)

Silence

Song of My Soul (Psalm 119)

Oh, how I love your law! all the day long it is in
my mind.
Your commandment has made me wiser than my
enemies,
and it is always with me.
I have more understanding than all my teachers,
for your decrees are my study.
I am wiser than the elders,
because I observe your commandments.
I restrain my feet from every evil way,
that I may keep your word.

I do not shrink from your judgments,
>because you yourself have taught me.
How sweet are your words to my taste!
>they are sweeter than honey to my mouth.
Through your commandments I gain understanding;
>therefore I hate every lying way. (vs. 97–104)

A READING FROM THE PROPHETS

The wisdom of the humble lifts their heads high, and seats them among the great. Do not praise individuals for their good looks, or loathe anyone because of appearance alone. The bee is small among flying creatures, but what it produces is the best of sweet things. . . . Many kings have had to sit on the ground, but one who was never thought of has worn a crown. (Sirach 11:1–3, 5)

NEW TESTAMENT READING

God chose those who by human standards are fools to shame the wise; he chose those who by human standards are weak to shame the strong, those who by human standards are common and contemptible— indeed those who count for nothing—to reduce to nothing all those that do count for something, so that no human being might feel boastful before God. It is by him that you exist in Christ Jesus, who for us was made wisdom from God, and saving justice and holiness and redemption. As scripture says: If anyone wants to boast, let him boast of the Lord. (1 Cor. 1:27–31)

Silence

AN EARLY FRANCISCAN SAYING

The brothers . . . should aim to maintain silence as long as God gives them the grace. They shouldn't argue among themselves or with others, but instead, should always be ready to humbly say, "We are worthless slaves!" They shouldn't be angry, for if you are angry you will be liable to judgement; if you insult, you will be liable to the council; and if you say, "You fool," you will be liable to the hell of fire. [Matt. 5:22]

—Francis of Assisi

A SPIRITUAL PRACTICE

Some of us need to practice humility desperately. There are many deliberately humiliating practices—such as those mentioned in the opening chapters from the Gospels and the lives of the Franciscan saints—and they do us much good. Find a way to deliberately humble yourself today. But others, perhaps, only need to be reminded that our humility is a virtue as we stand before God. Circumstances and life events have already, and thoroughly, brought us low. Such ones as these are like the poor whom Christ says will inherit the kingdom of God (Lk. 6:20). If this is you, simply know that you need to do nothing else to make yourself humble. For you, simply know that God sees each of us and knows who we are.

EVENING PRAYER
WEDNESDAY
Theme/Intent: Blessed Are the Humble

PREPARATION
In the dark of this night,
watch over me,
O Lord.
As I attempt to watch for You.
Amen.

THE WORD OF GOD
Jesus said to them, "In truth I tell you, tax collectors
and prostitutes are making their way into the kingdom of God before you." (Matt. 21:31)

Silence

Song of My Soul (Psalm 121)
I lift up my eyes to the hills;
    from where is my help to come?
My help comes from the LORD,
    the maker of heaven and earth.
He will not let your foot be moved
    and he who watches over you will not fall asleep.
Behold, he who keeps watch over Israel
    shall neither slumber nor sleep;
The LORD himself watches over you;
    the LORD is your shade at your right hand,
So that the sun shall not strike you by day,
    nor the moon by night.

The LORD shall preserve you from all evil;
　　it is he who shall keep you safe. (vs. 1–7)

A READING FROM THE PROPHETS

Woe to you who strive with your Maker, earthen
vessels with the potter! Does the clay say to the one
who fashions it, "What are you making"? or "Your
work has no handles"? Woe to anyone who says to
a father, "What are you begetting?" or to a woman,
"With what are you in labor?" Thus says the LORD,
the Holy One of Israel, and its Maker: Will you
question me? (Isa. 45:9–11)

NEW TESTAMENT READING

At this time the disciples came to Jesus and
said, "Who is the greatest in the kingdom of
Heaven?" So he called a little child to him whom
he set among them. Then he said, "In truth I
tell you, unless you change and become like
little children you will never enter the kingdom of
Heaven. And so, the one who makes himself as little
as this little child is the greatest in the kingdom of
Heaven. In truth I tell you, whatever you bind on
earth will be bound in heaven; whatever you loose
on earth will be loosed in heaven.
(Matt. 18:1–4, 18)

Silence

AN EARLY FRANCISCAN SAYING

Brothers, who is so noble that he wouldn't carry a basket of manure from St. Mary's all through town, if he were given a house of gold? Why don't we want to endure a little shame in order to gain eternal life?
—Brother Juniper[26]

A SPIRITUAL PRACTICE

Kneel to pray tonight, even if you haven't kneeled with spiritual intention for decades. Do it even if it feels odd. You aren't doing it to please God; you are doing it because your body can teach your soul something important.

THURSDAY

Theme/Intent: The Pure in Heart Are Blessed

PREPARATION
Show me today, Lord,
The beauty of Your foolishness,
How Yours are the ways that
lead to bliss.
I want bliss. I want You.
Amen.

THE WORD OF GOD
Blessed are the pure in heart: they shall see God.
(Matt. 5:8)

Silence

Song of My Soul (Psalm 131)
O LORD, I am not proud;
    I have no haughty looks.
I do not occupy myself with great matters,
    or with things that are too hard for me.
But I still my soul and make it quiet,
    like a child upon its mother's breast;
    my soul is quieted within me.
O Israel, wait upon the LORD,
    from this time forth for evermore.

A READING FROM THE PROPHETS

Morning by morning he wakens—wakens my ear to listen as those who are taught. The LORD God has opened my ear, and I was not rebellious, I did not turn backward. I gave my back to those who struck me, and my cheek to those who pulled out the beard; I did not hide my face from insult and spitting. (Isa. 50:4a–6)

NEW TESTAMENT READING

Blessed are the peacemakers: they shall be recognized
    as children of God.
Blessed are those who are persecuted in the cause of
    uprightness: the kingdom of Heaven is theirs.
Blessed are you when people abuse you and
    persecute you and speak all kinds
    of calumny against you falsely on my account.
Rejoice and be glad, for your reward will be great
    in heaven; this is how they persecuted the
    prophets before you. (Matt. 5:9–12)

Silence

AN EARLY FRANCISCAN SAYING

The brothers should all strive to follow the humility and poverty of our Lord Jesus Christ, and remember that we deserve nothing else in the whole world except what the apostle says: "if we have food and clothing, we will be content with these" [1 Tim. 6:8]. Similarly, they should rejoice when they have an opportunity to talk with people who are easily

despised, with the poor and the weak, with the sick and lepers, and with anyone who begs in the streets.
—Francis of Assisi

A SPIRITUAL PRACTICE

Good athletes and good musicians will tell you that there is a secret to their success that most coaches fail to teach well: getting out of the way. An athlete gets out of the way of her teammates so that they can make the shot or run with the baton. A musician takes himself out of the way and allows the instrument to shine, since that's what really matters. Look for ways today that you might get out of the way.

EVENING PRAYER
THURSDAY
Theme/Intent: The Pure in Heart Are Blessed

PREPARATION
I need nothing tonight but You,
Lord.
Your Presence.
Not Your protection (but I'll take it)!
I need Your love.

THE WORD OF GOD
Blessed are the pure in heart: they shall see God.
(Matt. 5:8)

Silence

Song of My Soul (Psalm 23)
The LORD is my shepherd; I shall not be in want.
He makes me lie down in green pastures
    and leads me beside still waters.
He revives my soul and guides me along right
    pathways for his Name's sake.
Though I walk through the valley of the shadow of
    death,I shall fear no evil; for you are with me;
    your rod and your staff, they comfort me.
You spread a table before me in the presence of
    those
who trouble me;
    you have anointed my head with oil,
    and my cup is running over.

Surely your goodness and mercy shall follow me
all the days of my life, and I will dwell in the
house of the LORD forever.

A READING FROM THE PROPHETS

The Lord GOD helps me; therefore I have not been
disgraced; therefore I have set my face like flint, and
I know that I shall not be put to shame; he who
vindicates me is near. Who will contend with me?
Let us stand up together. Who are my adversaries?
Let them confront me. It is the Lord GOD who
helps me. (Isa. 50:7–9)

NEW TESTAMENT READING

You are salt for the earth. But if salt loses its taste,
what can make it salty again? It is good for nothing, and can only be thrown out to be trampled
under people's feet. You are light for the world.
A city built on a hill-top cannot be hidden. No
one lights a lamp to put it under a tub; they put it
on the lamp-stand where it shines for everyone in
the house. In the same way your light must shine
in people's sight. (Matt. 5:13–16)

Silence

AN EARLY FRANCISCAN SAYING

The spirit of the Lord desires for our flesh to be
humiliated, lower, denied, considered by us as less
worthy. The spirit of the Lord desires humility and
patience, pure simplicity and peace of mind. It

desires, above all, righteous fear, holy wisdom, and the divine love of the Father, Son, and Holy Ghost.
—Francis of Assisi

A SPIRITUAL PRACTICE

Most of our parents taught us to do the opposite of what Francis of Assisi instructs in his Rule in the passage above. We are supposed to take good care of ourselves, and to present ourselves well in front of others. That's how we stay healthy and succeed. So, is Francis wrong? I don't think so. And our mothers weren't wrong, either—unless they taught us that we should *always* be in charge, or *always* seek our own way. Tomorrow, practice some small way of deliberate humility in your bearing, your appearance, your self-presentation. Ask God to show it to you. Maybe even—have fun with it.

FRIDAY
Theme/Intent: Folly Is Another Name for Righteousness

PREPARATION
I don't know what I'm doing
half the time, Lord,
but I know right now that I
want to do for You, today,
whatever I am supposed to do.
Show me, please.

THE WORD OF GOD
The message of the cross is folly for those who are
on the way to ruin, but for those of us who are on
the road to salvation it is the power of God.
(1 Cor. 1:18)

Silence

Song of My Soul (Psalm 113)
Hallelujah!
Give praise, you servants of the LORD;
praise the Name of the LORD.
Let the Name of the LORD be blessed,
from this time forth forevermore.
From the rising of the sun to its going down
let the Name of the LORD be praised.
He takes up the weak out of the dust
and lifts up the poor from the ashes.

He sets them with the princes,
with the princes of his people.
He makes a woman of a childless house
to be a joyful mother of children. (vs. 1–3, 6–8)

A READING FROM THE PROPHETS

Let justice roll down like waters, and righteousness
like an ever-flowing stream. (Amos 5:24)

NEW TESTAMENT READING

As scripture says: I am going to destroy the wisdom
of the wise and bring to nothing the understanding
of any who understand. Where are the philosophers?
Where are the experts? And where are the debaters
of this age? Do you not see how God has shown
up human wisdom as folly? Since in the wisdom
of God the world was unable to recognize God
through wisdom, it was God's own pleasure to save
believers through the folly of the gospel.
(1 Cor. 1:19–21)

Silence

AN EARLY FRANCISCAN SAYING

Unworthy servants of Christ as we are, may we sing
a new song in the presence of your holy presence
before your very throne, and follow the Lamb of
God wherever he goes.
—St. Clare of Assisi

A SPIRITUAL PRACTICE

Simply to be a healthy human being, we have to be able to laugh at ourselves. A holy fool does more than laugh: she tries to never take herself too seriously. Try clowning around this week, even if it doesn't feel comfortable at first. Learn to tell a joke. Wear something ridiculous. Smile at an inopportune time.

EVENING PRAYER
FRIDAY

*Theme/Intent: Folly Is another Name for Righteous-
ness*

PREPARATION

Is it possible, God,
that my life has
something to do with Yours?
I'm tired, and tonight, I don't know.
Is it okay for me to say just that?
But I want to know.
Amen.

THE WORD OF GOD

The message of the cross is folly for those who are
on the way to ruin, but for those of us who are on
the road to salvation it is the power of God.
(1 Cor. 1:18)

Silence

Song of My Soul (Psalm 139)

LORD, you have searched me out and known me;
you know my sitting down and my rising up;
you discern my thoughts from afar.
You trace my journeys and my resting-places
And are acquainted with all my ways.
Indeed, there is not a word on my lips,
But you, O LORD, know it altogether.

You press upon me behind and before
And lay your hand upon me.
Such knowledge is too wonderful. . . .
(vs. 1–5)

A READING FROM THE PROPHETS

Thus says the LORD: "Do not let the wise boast
in their wisdom, do not let the mighty boast in
their might, do not let the wealthy boast in their
wealth; but let those who boast boast in this, that
they understand and know me, that I am the LORD;
I act with steadfast love, justice, and righteousness in the earth, for in these things I delight, says
the LORD." (Jer. 9:23–24)

NEW TESTAMENT READING

We are preaching a crucified Christ . . . a Christ who
is both the power of God and the wisdom of God.
God's folly is wiser than human wisdom, and God's
weakness is stronger than human strength.
(1 Cor. 1:23–25)

Silence

AN EARLY FRANCISCAN SAYING

When we arrive and we're soaked by the rain and
chilled to the bone, completely drenched with mud
and very hungry, and we ring at the gate and the
brother on duty says, "Who are you? Go away!",
and we have to show patience and humility and
charity with someone whom God has made to say

what he says just to test us, write it down, brother: that's the source of our joy!
  —Francis of Assisi, speaking to Brother Leo

A SPIRITUAL PRACTICE

Most of us feel like we're too busy to play. Today is different. Do something you haven't done in ages, whether it's finding a swing set, playing catch, or rolling down a hill. See what playing can do for you (other than grass stains—don't worry about those, clothes can be washed), and see what it can do in your relationships with spouse, kids, neighbors, friends. Families, neighborhoods, and religious orders are not built on rules alone—they are built on friendships.

SATURDAY

Theme/Intent: True Wisdom Brings Peace and Justice

PREPARATION

I want to serve You, God,
and I think I know what to do.
What I need is courage, persistence,
and a touch of folly,
to get it done.
Make me conscious of You at my
side today. Amen.

THE WORD OF GOD

As scripture says: He traps the crafty in the snare
of their own cunning and again: The Lord knows
the plans of the wise and how insipid they are.
(1 Cor. 3:20)

Silence

Song of My Soul (Psalm 85)

Show us your mercy, O LORD,
and grant us your salvation.
I will listen to what the LORD God is saying,
for he is speaking peace to his faithful people
and to those who turn their hearts to him.
Truly, his salvation is very near to those who fear him,
that his glory may dwell in our land.
Mercy and truth have met together;
righteousness and peace have kissed each other.

Truth shall spring up from the earth,
  and righteousness shall look down from heaven.
(vs. 7–11)

A READING FROM THE PROPHETS

Shower, O heavens, from above, and let the skies rain down righteousness; let the earth open, that salvation may spring up, and let it cause righteousness to sprout up also; I the LORD have created it. Woe to you who strive with your Maker, earthen vessels with the potter! Does the clay say to the one who fashions it, "What are you making"? or "Your work has no handles"? (Isa. 45:8–9)

NEW TESTAMENT READING

He has given us an even greater grace, as scripture says: God opposes the proud but he accords his favor to the humble. Give in to God, then; resist the devil, and he will run away from you. The nearer you go to God, the nearer God will come to you. Clean your hands, you sinners, and clear your minds, you waverers. . . . Humble yourselves before the Lord and he will lift you up. (Jas. 4:6–8, 10)

Silence

AN EARLY FRANCISCAN SAYING

The word of God belongs not to the one who hears or speaks it, but to the one who does it.
—Brother Giles of Assisi

A SPIRITUAL PRACTICE

A holy fool loves extravagantly. She doesn't measure risks when giving to a homeless person. He forgives someone who slighted him without conditions or caveats. Search your heart today for someone you know is in need, or who needs to know that you forgive them. Show him or her your love in an extravagant way.

EVENING PRAYER
SATURDAY
Theme/Intent: True Wisdom Brings Peace and Justice

PREPARATION

O Lord, I want
Your kingdom,
on earth as it is in heaven.
I want it now, in my lifetime,
which means that I want
to help you bring it about
today. Amen.

THE WORD OF GOD

As scripture says: He traps the crafty in the snare
of their own cunning and again: The Lord knows
the plans of the wise and how insipid they are.
(1 Cor. 3:20)

Silence

Song of My Soul (Psalm 98)

Sing to the LORD a new song,
    for he has done marvelous things.
Sing to the LORD with the harp,
    with the harp and the voice of song.
With trumpets and the sound of the horn
    shout with joy before the King, the LORD.
Let the sea make a noise and all that is in it,
    the lands and those who dwell therein.

Let the rivers clap their hands,
>   and let the hills ring out with joy before the Lord,
>   when he comes to judge the earth.
In righteousness shall he judge the world
>   and the peoples with equity. (vs. 1, 6–10)

A READING FROM THE PROPHETS

The whole of wisdom is fear of the Lord. . . .
Better are the God-fearing who lack understanding
than the highly intelligent who transgress the law.
(Sirach 19:20, 24)

NEW TESTAMENT READING

The wisdom that comes down from above is
essentially something pure; it is also peaceable,
kindly and considerate; it is full of mercy and
shows itself by doing good; nor is there any trace
of partiality or hypocrisy in it. The peace sown by
peacemakers brings a harvest of justice.
(Jas. 3:17–18)

Silence

AN EARLY FRANCISCAN SAYING

Humility seems to me to be like lightning. As
lightning causes terrible flashes and nothing can
afterward be found of it, so does humility dissipate
every evil and is the foe of every sin, but leaves
nothing behind. —Brother Giles of Assisi

A SPIRITUAL PRACTICE

Where does God's love want to take you—today, someday soon, in the near future? Each of us, if we quiet our mind and listen, will eventually hear the Holy Spirit speak in our heart. What is God saying to you? Where does your foolish love need to take you?

IV
OCCASIONAL
PRAYERS
FOR FOOLS

Christian spirituality, prayer, and liturgy are replete with the words of holy fools down through the centuries. These are like pearls so precious that if a man or woman discovered one in a field they might go out and sell everything they own in order to buy that field.

Some are words composed by Christians who were holy fools; others are words that inspired and inspire holy fools, then and now. We are all on this journey together and certain prayers have a power to inspire, guide, challenge, and prod us along in a way that others don't as much. This short chapter is an offering of seventeen of these, many of them Franciscan, organized in no particular order.

These two prayers are slight variations on prayers in common use throughout Catholic and other Christian churches on the feast days of saints:

> O God, who has brought us near to an
>   innumerable
> company of angels and to the spirits of just
>   men and women made perfect: Grant
>   us during our earthly pilgrimage to
>   abide in
> their fellowship, and in our heavenly
>   country to become
> partakers of their joy; through Jesus Christ
>   our Lord, who
> liveth and reigneth with thee and the Holy
>   Spirit, one God,
> now and for ever. *Amen.*

O Almighty God, who by thy Holy Spirit
    has made us one
with thy saints in heaven and on earth:
    Grant that in our
earthly pilgrimage we may ever be
    supported by this
fellowship of love and prayer, and may
    know ourselves
to be surrounded by their witness to thy
    power and mercy.
We ask this for the sake of Jesus Christ, in
    whom all our
intercessions are acceptable through the
    Spirit, and who
liveth and reigneth for ever and ever. Amen.

This is the prayer that Francis is said to have prayed on the day he first heard God speaking to him. Francis was kneeling in the ruined church of San Damiano, outside the medieval walls of the hill-town of Assisi, in silence, alone, when God said in such a way that Francis could understand: "Go and rebuild my Church." Francis responded in his usual, literal way: by gathering bricks in town and reconstructing that very church. This prayer later became Francis's prayer for himself, as well as the spirit of the Franciscan movement. It is textual tradition for it to be laid out as verse, since Francis is widely recognized as one of the first authors of poetry in the Italian vernacular. The crucifix before which Francis prayed is actually an icon; it is the image of the crucifix painted onto a twelve-centimeters-thick block of wood in the shape of a cross. It hangs in the Basilica of Santa Clara in Assisi to this day.[31]

Most High,
Most glorious God,
Enlighten the shadows of my heart.
Grant me a right and true faith,
A certain hope, and
A perfect charity, feeling, and understanding
Of You,
So that I may be able to accomplish
Your holy and just commands.
Amen.

~~9

This is the traditional priestly blessing, found in Numbers 6:24–26, used often by Francis and millions of other Christians throughout the ages:

> The Lord bless you and keep you;
> the Lord make his face to shine upon you,
> and be gracious to you;
> the Lord lift up his countenance upon you,
> and give you peace.

~❍

This is Francis of Assisi's version of The Lord's Prayer that extends and expands it, a sign of his great enthusiasm for the most important prayer of Christ.

Our Father,
Most Holy, our Creator and Redeemer, our Savior and our Comforter.

Who art in heaven
Together with the angels and the saints, giving them light so that they may have knowledge of you, because you, Lord, are Light; inflaming them so that they may love, because you, Lord, are Love; living continually in them and filling them so that they may be happy, because you, Lord, are the supreme good, the eternal good, and it is from you that all good comes, and without you there is no good.

Hallowed be thy name.
May our knowledge of you become ever clearer, so that we may realize the width and breadth of your blessings, the steadfastness of your promises, the sublimity of your majesty, and the depth of your judgments.

Thy kingdom come,
So that you may reign in us by your grace and
bring us to your Kingdom, where we will see
you clearly, love you perfectly, be blessed in your
presence, and enjoy you forever.

Thy will be done on earth as it is in heaven:
So that we may love you with our whole heart
by always thinking of you; directing our whole
intention with our whole mind toward you and
seeking your glory in everything; spending all
our powers and affections of soul and body with
all our strength in the service of your love alone.
May we also love our neighbors as ourselves,
encouraging them to love you as best we can,
rejoicing at the good fortune of others, just as
if it were our own, and sympathizing with their
misfortunes, giving offense to no one.

Give us this day our daily bread,
Your own beloved Son, our Lord Jesus Christ,
so to remind us of the love he showed for us
and to help us understand and appreciate it and
everything that he did or said or suffered.

And forgive us our trespasses,
In your infinite mercy, and by the power of
the Passion of your Son, our Lord Jesus Christ,
together with the merits and the intercession of
the Blessed Virgin Mary and all your saints.

As we forgive those who trespass against us,
And if we do not forgive perfectly, Lord, make us
do so, so that we may indeed love our enemies out
of our love for you, and pray fervently to you for
them, never returning evil for evil, anxious only to
serve everybody in you.

And lead us not into temptation.
Neither hidden or obvious, sudden or unforeseen.

But deliver us from evil—
Present, past, or to come. Amen.

~9

F rancis and Juniper, like all the early Franciscans and most of the saints before and after them, maintained a great daily devotion to the Blessed Virgin Mary.

The Hail Mary
Hail Mary, full of grace. The Lord is with thee.

Blessed art thou amongst women,

and blessed is the fruit of thy womb, Jesus.

Holy Mary, Mother of God,

pray for us sinners,

now and at the hour of our death. Amen.

The Memorare
Remember, O most gracious Virgin Mary,

that never was it known

that any one who fled to thy protection,

implored thy help

or sought thy intercession,

was left unaided.

Inspired by this confidence,

We fly unto thee, O Virgin of virgins my
    Mother;
        to thee do we come, before thee we
        stand, sinful and sorrowful;

O Mother of the Word Incarnate,

despise not our petitions,

but in thy mercy hear and answer them.
    Amen.

The Angelus

The Angel of the Lord declared to
Mary: and she conceived of the Holy
Spirit.

Hail Mary, full of grace, the Lord is with
you; blessed are you among women and
blessed is the fruit of your womb, Jesus.
Holy Mary, Mother of God, pray for
us sinners, now and at the hour of our
death. Amen.

Behold the handmaid of the Lord: Be it
done unto me according to your word.

[Repeat the opening prayer, above] Hail Mary
. . .

And the Word was made flesh: and dwelt
among us.

[Again, repeat] Hail Mary . . .

Pray for us, O Holy Mother of God, that
we may be made worthy of the promises of Christ.

We pray:

Pour forth, we beg you, O Lord, your grace
into our hearts; that we, to whom the
incarnation of Christ, your Son, was
made known by the message of an
angel, may by his passion and cross be
brought to the glory of his resurrection,
through the same Christ our Lord.
Amen.

The Glory Be
Glory be to the Father,
and to the Son,
and to the Holy Spirit,
as it was in the beginning,
is now, and ever shall be,
world without end. Amen.

~ひ~

Written as it was in the year 1225, when the regard for physical creation was as low as it has been at any time in history, Francis's famous "Canticle of the Creatures" astounds. Only today, with the benefit of the teachings of physician-priest Teilhard de Chardin, the poems of Mary Oliver and Wendell Berry, and the encyclical of Pope Francis, *Laudato Si*, has this incredibly foolish prayer of Francis's from eight hundred years ago finally come of age.

Most high, almighty, good Lord God,
    To you belong all praise, honor, and blessing!
Praised be you, O my Lord and God, with all your
    creatures,
    And especially our Brother Sun,
    Who brings us the day and who brings us the
    light.
He is fair and shines with a very great splendor:
    O Lord, he signifies you to us!
Praised be you, Most High, for Sister Moon and
    the Stars,
    You set them in the heavens, making them so
    Bright, luminous, and fine.
Praised be you, O my Lord, for our Brother Wind,
    And for air and cloud, calms and all weather

By whom you uphold life in all creatures.
Praise the Lord for our Sister Water,
    Who is very useful to us and humble
    And precious and clean.
Praise the Lord for our Brother Fire,
    Through whom you give us light in the
    darkness.
He is bright and pleasant and very mighty and
    strong.
Praise the Lord for our Mother Earth,
    Who sustains us and keeps us,
    And brings forth the grass and all
    Of the fruits and flowers of many colors.
Praised be you, O my Lord, for all who show
    forgiveness and
    Pardon one another for your sake,
    And who endure weakness and tribulation.
Blessed are they who peaceably endure,
For you, Most High, shall give them a crown.
Praise to you, O my Lord, for our Sister Death
    And the death of the body from whom no one
    may escape.
Woe to those who die in mortal sin,
    But blessed as they who are found walking by
    your most
    Holy will,
For the second death
    Shall have no power to do them any harm.
Praise to you, O my Lord, and all blessing.
We give you thanks and serve you with great
    humility.

~ひ

Lord,
without your hand
I can do nothing.
—Brother Juniper

~ひ

O my most sweet Lord Jesus Christ,
have pity on me and on my Lady Poverty,
for I burn with love for her, and without her
I cannot rest.
O my Lord, who did cause me to love her,
you know that she is sitting in sadness,
rejected by all.
—Francis of Assisi, in the paraphrase of
    Blessed Frederick Ozanam (1813–1853)

This, then, is what I pray, kneeling before the Father, from whom every fatherhood, in heaven or on earth, takes its name. In the abundance of his glory may he, through his Spirit, enable you to grow firm in power with regard to your inner self, so that Christ may live in your hearts through faith, and then, planted in love and built on love, with all God's holy people you will have the strength to grasp the breadth and the length, the height and the depth; so that, knowing the love of Christ, which is beyond knowledge, you may be filled with the utter fullness of God.

—Ephesians 3:14–19

The Sanctus (inspired by Isaiah 6:3)
Holy, Holy, Holy Lord God of hosts.
Heaven and earth are full of your glory.
Hosanna in the highest.
Blessed is he who comes in the name of the Lord.
Hosanna in the highest.

~◠

Traditional prayer after baptism from the early
church:

O God, God of truth, God of the whole
universe,

God of all creation, fill this your servant
with your blessing and keep him as
clean as his new birth had left him.

May he share the lot of your angelic
powers and henceforth be called not
flesh but spirit, for the gift he has
received from you is divine and of
sovereign efficacy.

May he be kept safe for you to the end,
Creator of all that is, through your
only Son, Jesus Christ.

Through him may glory and power be
yours, age after age. Amen.

There might be no more powerful prayer from the saints before St. Francis than this prayer to God the Holy Spirit attributed to St. Augustine of Hippo:

> Breathe in me, O Holy Spirit,
> That my thoughts may all be holy.
> Act in me, O Holy Spirit,
> That my work, too, may be holy.
> Draw my heart, O Holy Spirit,
> That I may love only what is holy.
> Strengthen me, O Holy Spirit,
> To defend all that is holy.
> Guard me, then, O Holy Spirit,
> That I always may be holy.

~⌒

Almighty, eternal, just, and merciful God,
grant to us miserable ones the grace to do
for you what we know you want us to do.
Give us always to desire what pleases You.
Inwardly cleansed, interiorly illumined and
enflamed with the fire of the Holy Spirit,
may we be able to follow in the footprints of your
beloved Son, our Lord Jesus Christ, and attain
to you, Most High, by your grace alone, who
in perfect Trinity and simple Unity lives
and reigns and is glorified as God almighty,
forever and ever. Amen.
—Francis of Assisi

V

FOUR STORIES
of BROTHER JUNIPER
from *The Little Flowers*

We tend to know many of the stories about Francis of Assisi. Or at least, they are easily obtainable. Brother Juniper is less known. The stories from his life are always colorful, countercultural (even among his fellow friars), and they deserve to be better known. Here are four of them.

WHEN JUNIPER WENT
NAKED TO TOWN

One day, Brother Juniper wished to completely humiliate himself. So he stripped his body of all of its clothes. Completely naked and exposed, Juniper put his underwear like a hat upon his head and tied his friar's habit with its cord around his neck, like a scarf. Done up in this way, he walked into Viterbo, straight into the town market, anxious to be mocked.

There in the marketplace he sat, in his nakedness, for only a few minutes before some youths saw him and decided he was surely insane. They began to throw rocks and mud at him, and they insulted him in every way they could think of. They even began to push him around.

Juniper smiled at them, and his smiles only seemed to inflame the boys' worst behavior.

After more than an hour of this, Juniper was a mess, and also a bit hurt. He decided to leave the city center and walk back to the friary that was already in that town.

When the other friars saw him, they were shocked and concerned, but they were also angry with Juniper for embarrassing the friary before the whole town, as he had done. "Let's lock him up!" one of them said, referring to how Francis had once written that a heretical friar could be locked up in a prison in the friary, if necessary, before sending him away for religious discipline.

"He should actually be hanged!" another friar yelled, surely in half-jest, but also demonstrating how upset they all were with their brother.

"Maybe even burned at the stake!" added another, in the same spirit.

"No penalty is too great for how this man has betrayed our blessed Order! He has proven to be a shocking example of what it means to be a friar of God in this town," someone said.

Brother Juniper was sitting quietly and smiling while listening to this barrage. When they were all done, they demanded an answer from him. What led him to do such a thing in Viterbo? Finally, he smiled and answered them all, with joy and humility.

"All of you are right," he said, "I deserve everything you say, and even more for what I have done."

This was all to the glory of Christ. Amen.

WHEN JUNIPER
COOKED
FOR THE FRIARS

There was once a time when Juniper was the only friar staying behind in the friary. All of the other friars were heading out for the day. The guardian said to him, "Brother, will you please prepare some food for the friars, so they can eat upon their return?" "I'll be happy to do so," Juniper replied. Then, the other friars went out.

Juniper began to think about the task at hand. *What a shame it is*, he thought to himself, *that every day one of the friars has to occupy so much of his time with cooking instead of praying. I think I will cook enough today to last the friars for two weeks!*

And so Juniper went into town and began to beg. He needed pots for cooking, and he wished to have eggs, meat, and some vegetables. On his way back to the friary, he also stopped to gather some firewood.

He filled the pots with water and put them over a fire that he made. Then he placed everything he'd received into the pots: vegetables, uncut; chickens, still with their feathers; and dozens of eggs, in their shells. *Everything will cook together, all at once!* he thought.

Once everything was underway, one of the other friars came home early. Juniper let him in and together they sat by the roaring cook-fire. This other friar was one who loved Juniper for his simple ways, but he began to ponder what was in the pots and to observe what Juniper had underway. The big pots were so hot that he didn't dare go near them; in fact, he covered up so as not be get burned from the heat they were throwing off. Juniper, meanwhile, remained busy stirring the contents and adding wood to the fires. A few hours later, all the friars returned to the friary. "Brother Juniper is definitely preparing a feast for us!" said the first friar to all the others.

Juniper rang the bell for supper and the brothers filed into the refectory. Juniper's face was red from the heat and exhaustion; he said, "Eat well, brothers, and then let's go pray. And no one should have to cook again for two weeks!"

The friars sat and stared at the food put before them. They were dumbfounded, and refused to eat. Juniper picked up a boiled chicken with its feathers still on, and ripped off a bite of the most offensive-looking portion, saying, while choking on it, "This is good!"

The friars sat and stared at Juniper. They were amazed. Then the guardian began to scold him for his wastefulness and foolishness. "Don't you know . . ." he began to say. But then Juniper threw himself onto his knees and began to confess his sins to the gathering, chronicling nearly every sinful thing that he had said, done, and intended over the course of his life. "I have wasted so many good things of God and this Order!" Juniper moaned. And he wouldn't stop repenting.

Finally, the guardian said to the friars, "I wish that Juniper would waste every day what he wasted today, if we would then receive this sort of edification. His simplicity and charity made him do what he did here today."

WHY JUNIPER
PLAYED ON A SEESAW
IN ROME

It was several years after Brother Juniper had joined the Order, after his reputation was already well established, that he went to stay for a time in Rome. He was said to be a holy man, and there were some Romans who knew he was coming to their city, so they went out to meet him. Juniper saw these Romans on the road up ahead, awaiting him, and he wanted none of their devotion. He began to ponder how to turn their expectations, and this greeting, around.

At about that moment Juniper saw two boys playing on a seesaw, which they'd made by setting a board of wood over the top of a log, with one of them sitting at either end upon it. He walked up to the boys and smiled at them and asked to join in their play. Soon, Juniper was taking a turn and seesawing on one end, a boy on the other. His arms were in the air and he was laughing like a child himself.

The crowd of expectant Romans saw this and they began to come closer. They wanted to take Juniper into the city, to honor him, and to show him where a man of holiness could lie down and rest after such a journey. But Juniper kept on playing.

The people were gobsmacked. As Juniper laughed and waved his arms, the people were trying to reverence and greet him as the holy man they knew he was supposed to be. But Juniper wanted to turn their reverencing into mocking and scorn.

"He's a fool," one of the Romans then finally said. Others were not sure. But, as Juniper kept on playing with the boys on the seesaw rather than listening to the crowd that had come to greet him, after a little while all the Romans slowly wandered away, disappointed. It was only then that Brother Juniper stopped seesawing and eventually made his way, quietly and on his own, to the friary in Rome.

HOW JUNIPER BECAME RAPT WITH ECSTASY ONE DAY AT MASS

Juniper was not a priest. He never said Mass, but he always listened to the Mass with close attention. At Mass, he was always devout within himself and composed in the presence of others.

But one day, when Juniper was at Mass at St. Mary of the Angels—the Portiuncula—he slowly became rapt with a kind of ecstasy. The look on his face showed that he had been transported, as if to another place. His brothers saw this and realized he had become unresponsive, so when the Mass came to an end they left him in the chapel.

After a long while, Juniper returned to his usual senses. Realizing that he was still kneeling in the corner of the Portiuncula, he rose and went to find his brothers outside. He was excited, bursting with his usual exuberance.

"Brothers!" he called as he approached them. They saw that he had returned from his state.

"Who in this life of ours is so noble that he wouldn't carry a basket of pig manure from St. Mary's all through the town of Assisi in order to earn a basketful of gold?" he said.

They smiled. Everyone would.

"In the same way," Juniper went on, for this is what he heard from God on his knees, "why don't we all want to endure brief moments of shame in order to gain life eternal, which is better and lasts longer than any gold in the world?!"

ACKNOWLEDGMENTS

This is my third book of this kind. The first, *The St. Francis Prayer Book*, was published in 2004. It was then followed by *The St. Clare Prayer Book* in 2007. A decade later and now we have a trinity, so to speak, adding the charism of Francis and Juniper to the earlier Franciscan foundations. That's as it should be, I think—moving on to holy foolery only after we have immersed ourselves in all the themes that gave rise to the Franciscan reforms in the first place.

What a pleasure these books have been in my life! I express heartfelt thanks to all the editors with whom I've worked on these little gems at Paraclete Press over the years: Lillian Miao, Ron Minor, Carol Showalter, Pamela Jordan, Sr. Mercy Minor, Robert Edmonson, and Phil Fox Rose.

NOTES

xiii *Angels can fly*   G. K. Chesterton, *Orthodoxy*, 1908, various editions.

xvii *I give you the end of a golden string*   William Blake, *Jerusalem: The Emanation of the Giant Albion*, 1804–1820, plate 77, 1–4.

xix *Someone among them remarked*   From "The Anonymous of Perugia," in *Francis of Assisi: Early Documents,* Vol. II, eds. Regis J. Armstrong OFM Cap, J.A. Wayne Hellman, OFM Conv, and William J. Short, OFM (New York: New City Press, 2000), 43.

xix *Jugglers for God*   A rich tradition of holy foolishness exists in the Russian Orthodox tradition; its character is different from that in the West, exemplified by Francis and Juniper. In both traditions, following the humility of Christ is essential, but among Russian saints, a fool is never feebleminded; he is often meant to irritate, exasperate, and provoke others to see the errors of conventional understanding.

xx *The truth is that when his mind was completely gone* Miguel de Cervantes, *Don Quixote*, a new translation by Edith Grossman (New York: Ecco, 2005), 21.

xxiii *The whole secret of mysticism is this*   Chesterton, *Orthodoxy*. In this quote, may GKC forgive me, I have altered his masculine pronouns to make the message more universal.

xxiii *One must seek for the truth of things*   Miguel de Unamuno, *The Private World: Selections from the Diario*

Intimo and Selected Letters 1890-1936, trans. By Martin Nozick with Allen Lacy (Princeton: Princeton University Press, 1984), 3.

xxiv *this joy to be shown through laughter or even empty words* Francis of Assisi: Early Documents, Vol. III, eds. Regis J. Armstrong OFM Cap, J.A. Wayne Hellman, OFM Conv, and William J. Short, OFM (New York: New City Press, 2001), 343.

xxv *I have found both freedom and safety in my madness* From The Madman: His Parables and Poems, first published in 1918. See Kahlil Gibran, The Collected Works (New York: Everyman's Library, 2007), 5.

4 *Let's lock him up* Paraphrased from an account in The Little Flowers of St. Francis. This story does not appear in my book, The Complete Francis of Assisi: His Life, the Complete Writings, and The Little Flowers (Brewster, MA: Paraclete Press, 2015).

5 *It was in the days when Francis* Brother Ugolino, comp., The Little Flowers of Saint Francis, arranged chronologically and rendered into contemporary English by Jon M. Sweeney (Brewster, MA: Paraclete Press, 2016), 5.

5 *Almost up to the twenty-fifth year of his age* Thomas of Celano, First Life, 2; Habig, Omnibus, 230.

6 *His armor being now furbished* Miguel de Cervantes, Don Quixote, trans. Charles Jarvis, edited by Lester G. Crocker (New York: Washington Square Press, 1970), 5.

7 *You are right!* From "The Legend of Three Companions," in *Francis of Assisi: Early Documents,* Vol. II, 72.

8 *I never thought of it before* Murray Bodo, *Juniper: Friend of Francis, Fool of God* (Cincinnati: St. Anthony Messenger Press, 1983), 12.

9 *The Sufi poet Rumi once told a story* Other than this quote, I'm paraphrasing the fable; but see "The policeman and the drunkard, on spiritual intoxication," in *Tales from the Masnavi,* A. J. Arberry; London: George Allen and Unwin, 1961; 152-3.

20 *As I continued to meet holy fools* Mathew Woodley, *Holy Fools: Following Jesus with Reckless Abandon* (Carol Stream, IL: Saltriver/Tyndale House, 2008), 63.

22 *How foolish to be an unholy fool!* Elizabeth-Anne Stewart, *Jesus the Holy Fool* (Sheed & Ward, 1999), 32.

22 *If one does not understand the usefulness of the useless* Eugene Ionesco, quoted in Thomas Merton's essay, "Rain and the Rhinoceros," in *Raids on the Unspeakable* (New York: New Directions, 1966), 21.

23 *A change of heart or of values without a practice* Wendell Berry, *In the Presence of Fear: Three Essays for a Changed World* (Great Barrington, MA: The Orion Society, 2001), 13.

31 *As you announce peace with your mouth* From "The Legend of Three Companions," in *Francis of Assisi: Early Documents,* Vol. II, 102.

35   *The sisters shall not acquire anything as their own*   From Clare's Rule, para. 8, in *Francis and Clare: The Complete Works*, trans. Regis J. Armstrong, OFM Cap and Ignatius C. Brady, OFM (New York: Paulist Press, 1982), 219-220.

41   *The brothers should always be careful*   Francis of Assisi, The Original Rule, para. 7. See *The Complete Francis of Assisi*, ed. Jon M. Sweeney (Brewster, MA: Paraclete Press, 2015), 213.

44   *Sinners will come back to their God by humility*   From *The Little Flowers*, in *The Complete Francis of Assisi*, 336.

47   *The brothers . . . should aim to maintain silence*   Francis of Assisi, The Original Rule, para. 11, slightly modified. See *The Complete Francis of Assisi*, 216.

50   *Brothers, who is so noble*   My translation from *The Little Flowers*. Not included in *The Complete Francis of Assisi*.

53   *The brothers should all strive*   Francis of Assisi, The Original Rule, para. 9. See *The Complete Francis of Assisi*, 214.

56   *The spirit of the Lord desires for our flesh to be humiliated* Francis of Assisi, The Original Rule, para. 17. See *The Complete Francis of Assisi*, 220.

58   *Unworthy servants of Christ as we are*   From the fourth letter that Clare wrote to Agnes. First appeared in slightly different form in *The St. Clare Prayer Book* (Brewster, MA: Paraclete Press, 2007), 112.

61   *When we arrive and we're soaked by the rain*   Slightly adapted from *The Little Flowers*. See *The Complete Francis of Assisi*, 341.

74　*This is the prayer that Francis is said to have prayed*
　　Slightly adapted from *The Complete Francis of Assisi*, 205.

77　*This is Francis of Assisi's version of The Lord's Prayer*
　　Slightly adapted from *The Complete Francis of Assisi*,
　　256–7.

88　*Traditional prayer after Baptism*　　From *Early Christian Prayers*, ed. A. Hamman, OFM, trans. Walter Mitchell (Chicago: Henry Regnery, 1961), 128.

90　*Almighty, eternal, just, and merciful God*　　Taken from *The St. Francis Prayer Book: A Guide to Deepen Your Spiritual Life* (Brewster, MA: Paraclete Press, 2004), 126.

93　*Here are four [stories from Brother Juniper's life]*
　　These translations are original. The stories of Juniper were not included in my earlier work, *The Little Flowers of Saint Francis*, which was published in hardcover in 2011 by Paraclete Press, and then issued in paperback in 2016.

INDEX OF SCRIPTURES

Matthew: **5:8–16** (51, 52, 54, 55); **5:22** (47); **5:27–28** (xvi); **6:19–22** (xxii, 31); **18:1–4, 18** (49); **21:31** (45, 48).

Mark: **3:21** (xvi); **15:1–5** (37).

Luke: **6:20** (47); **9:3** (xxii); **9:58** (8); **15:3–7** (40).

John: **19:1–5** (34).

Philippians: **2:7** (22); **4:4–8** (43).

1 Corinthians: **1:18–21** (21, 23, 57, 58, 60); **1:23–25** (61); **1:27–31** (46); **3:19** (33, 36); **3:20** (63, 66); **4:10** (xiv, 27, 30); **4:9–13** (29).

Ephesians: **3:14–19** (87).

1 Thessalonians: **5:19** (39, 42).

1 Timothy: **6:8** (52).

James: **3:17–18** (67); **4:6–10** (64).

ABOUT PARACLETE PRESS

Who We Are

Paraclete Press is a publisher of books, recordings, and DVDs on Christian spirituality. Our publishing represents a full expression of Christian belief and practice—from Catholic to Evangelical, from Protestant to Orthodox.

We are the publishing arm of the Community of Jesus, an ecumenical monastic community in the Benedictine tradition. As such, we are uniquely positioned in the marketplace without connection to a large corporation and with informal relationships to many branches and denominations of faith.

What We Are Doing

PARACLETE PRESS BOOKS | Paraclete publishes books that show the richness and depth of what it means to be Christian. Although Benedictine spirituality is at the heart of all that we do, we publish books that reflect the Christian experience across many cultures, time periods, and houses of worship. We publish books that nourish the vibrant life of the church and its people.

We have several different series, including the best-selling Paraclete Essentials and Paraclete Giants series of classic texts in contemporary English; Voices from the Monastery—men and women monastics writing about living a spiritual life today; award-winning poetry; best-selling gift books for children on the occasions of baptism and first communion; and the Active Prayer Series that brings creativity and liveliness to any life of prayer.

MOUNT TABOR BOOKS | Paraclete's newest series, Mount Tabor Books, focuses on the arts and literature as well as liturgical worship and spirituality, and was created in conjunction with the Mount Tabor Ecumenical Centre for Art and Spirituality in Barga, Italy.

PARACLETE RECORDINGS | From Gregorian chant to contemporary American choral works, our recordings celebrate the best of sacred choral music composed through the centuries that create a space for heaven and earth to intersect. Paraclete Recordings is the record label representing the internationally acclaimed choir Gloriæ Dei Cantores, praised for their "rapt and fathomless spiritual intensity" by *American Record Guide*; the Gloriæ Dei Cantores Schola, specializing in the study and performance of Gregorian chant; and the other instrumental artists of the Arts Empowering Life Foundation.

Paraclete Press is also privileged to be the exclusive North American distributor of the recordings of the Monastic Choir of St. Peter's Abbey in Solesmes, France, long considered to be a leading authority on Gregorian chant.

PARACLETE VIDEO | Our DVDs offer spiritual help, healing, and biblical guidance for a broad range of life issues including grief and loss, marriage, forgiveness, facing death, bullying, addictions, Alzheimer's, and spiritual formation.

Learn more about us at our website:

www.paracletepress.com or phone us

SCAN
TO
READ
MORE

The St. Francis Prayer Book
A Guide to Deepen Your Spiritual Life
Jon M. Sweeney
978-1-55725-352-1 $16.99

This warm-hearted little book is a window into the soul of St. Francis, one of the most passionate and inspiring followers of Jesus. "Prayer was to Francis as play is to a child: natural, easy, creative, and joyful."

- Pray the words that Francis taught his spiritual brothers and sisters to pray.
- Explore Francis's time and place and feel the joy and earnestness of the first Franciscans.
- Experience how it is possible to live a contemplative and active life at the same time.

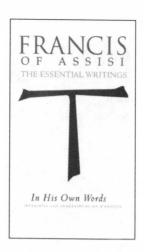

Francis of Assisi in His Own Words
The Essential Writings
Jon M. Sweeney
978-1-61261-069-6 $15.99

Biographies will only take you so far. It's impossible to truly understand Francis of Assisi without reading his writings. Sweeney has compiled all of the ones that we are most certain come from Francis himself, including his first Rule of life, the Rule he wrote for the Third Order, letters to friends, letters to people in power, messages to all Franciscans, songs, praises, canticles, and his final spiritual testament. An introduction and explanatory notes throughout the book help put the writings into historical and theological context.

Available through your local bookseller or through Paraclete Press: www.paracletepress.com; 1-800-451-5006